NATIVE AMERICAN PEOPLES

INVESTIGATE!

THE CHEYENNE

BY JOHN O'MARA

Enslow PUBLISHING

Please visit our website, www.enslow.com. For a free color catalog of all our high-quality books, call toll free 1-800-398-2504 or fax 1-877-980-4454.

Library of Congress Cataloging-in-Publication Data
Names: O'Mara, John, author.
Title: The Cheyenne / John O'Mara.
Other titles: Native American peoples.
Description: New York : Enslow Publishing, [2022] | Series: Native American peoples | Includes index.
Identifiers: LCCN 2020028563 (print) | LCCN 2020028564 (ebook) | ISBN 9781978521841 (library binding) | ISBN 9781978521827 (paperback) | ISBN 9781978521834 (set) | ISBN 9781978521858 (ebook)
Subjects: LCSH: Cheyenne Indians–Juvenile literature. | Cheyenne Indians–History–Juvenile literature.
Classification: LCC E99.C53 O43 2022 (print) | LCC E99.C53 (ebook) | DDC 978.004/97353–dc23
LC record available at https://lccn.loc.gov/2020028563
LC ebook record available at https://lccn.loc.gov/2020028564

Published in 2022 by
Enslow Publishing
29 E. 21st Street
New York, NY 10010

Designer: Katelyn E. Reynolds
Interior Layout: Tanya Dellaccio
Editor: Therese Shea

Photo credits: Cover, p. 1 (texture) aopsan/Shutterstock.com; cvr, pp. 1–24 (striped texture) Eky Studio/Shutterstock.com; pp. 4, 13, 15 (top left), 23 (top) Buyenlarge/ArchivePhotos/Getty Images; pp. 5, 19 (map) Kolonko/iStock/Getty Images Plus/Getty Images; p. 7 (left) duncan1890/DigitalVision Vectors/Getty Images; pp. 7 (right), 9 (left), 23 (bottom) Werner Forman/Universal Images Groups/Getty Images; p. 8 Wonwoo Lee/Image Source/Getty Images; p. 9 (right) UniversalImagesGroup/Getty Images; p. 12 Universal History Archive/Universal Images Group/Getty Images; p. 15 (bottom left) Library of Congress/Corbis Historical/Getty Images; p. 15 (right) https://upload.wikimedia.org/wikipedia/commons/4/4d/Ball_players.jpg; p. 16 https://upload.wikimedia.org/wikipedia/commons/0/0d/Native_American_PowWow_9488.jpg; p. 17 Historical/Corbis Historical/Getty Images; p. 19 (top left) https://upload.wikimedia.org/wikipedia/commons/d/db/Sun_Sign.jpg; p. 19 (bottom left) MPI/Archive Photos/Getty Images; p. 20 https://upload.wikimedia.org/wikipedia/commons/e/e6/George_Catlin_-_Né-hee-ó-ee-wóo-tis,_Wolf_on_the_Hill,_Chief_of_the_Tribe_-_1985.66.143_-_Smithsonian_American_Art_Museum.jpg; p. 21 Sepia Times/Universal Images Group/Getty Images; p. 24 DEA PICTURE LIBRARY/De Agostini/Getty Images; p. 25 Kean Collection/Archive Photos/Getty Images; p. 27 Education Images/Universal Images Group/Getty Images; p. 29 (both) J Pat Carter/Getty Images News.

Portions of this work were originally authored by Shalini Saxena and published as *The Cheyenne People*. All new material this edition authored by John O'Mara.

Printed in the United States of America

CPSIA compliance information: Batch #CSENS22: For further information contact Enslow Publishing, New York, New York, at 1-800-398-2504.

CONTENTS

WORDS IN THE GLOSSARY APPEAR IN BOLD TYPE THE FIRST TIME THEY ARE USED IN THE TEXT.

MEET THE CHEYENNE

The Cheyenne (shy-AN) people are a group of Native Americans with a rich **culture**. In the 1500s, the Cheyenne lived in today's Minnesota. They farmed, hunted, and gathered food.

GET THE FACTS!

By 1832, the Cheyenne separated into two groups. The Northern Cheyenne kept their hunting way of life near the Platte River in Wyoming. The Southern Cheyenne became more settled along the Arkansas River in Colorado. They kept in touch, however.

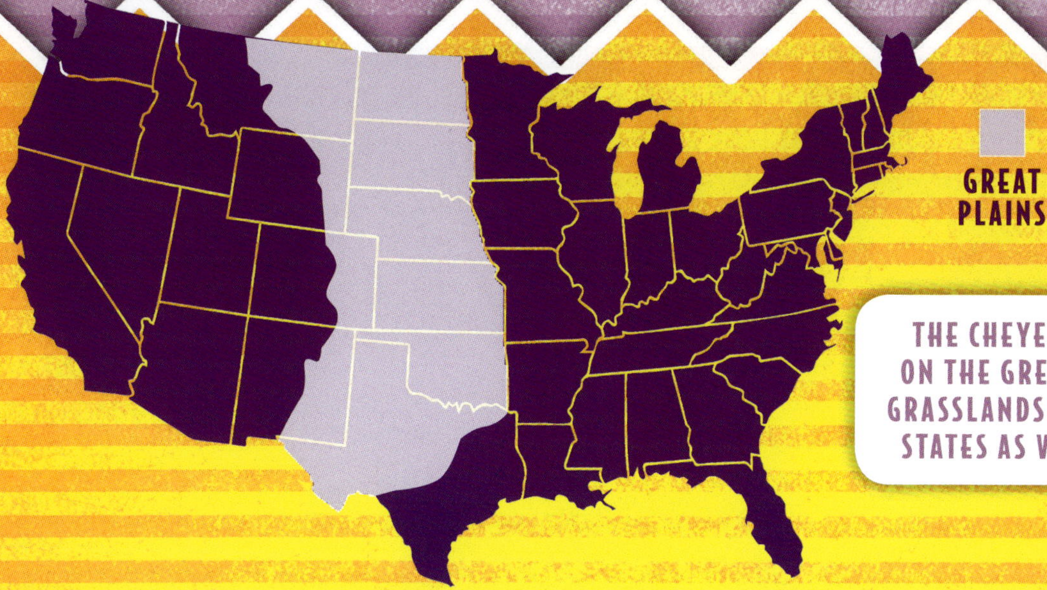

THE CHEYENNE HAD A LONG HISTORY ON THE GREAT PLAINS. THIS RANGE OF GRASSLANDS INCLUDES PARTS OF 10 U.S. STATES AS WELL AS AREAS OF CANADA.

In the 1700s, the Cheyenne moved to the area that's now North Dakota and South Dakota. Some groups continued to farm. Others became hunters, following herds of bison. At its largest, Cheyenne hunting territory reached from Montana in the north to Texas in the south. Wars with other Native Americans and settlers shrunk their territory in the Great Plains.

CHEYENNE HOMES

The Cheyenne built homes that fit their way of life. When they were farmers, they stayed in one place. So, they built homes that could last a long time. These were earth lodges, which meant they were partly or wholly covered by earth, or soil.

After the Cheyenne started hunting bison, they needed homes they could carry as they followed the herds. Tepees, or tipis, were the answer. These cone-shaped tents were made of wooden poles and bison hide. A village of tepees could be packed up within hours.

THIS TEPEE MODEL USES A BISON HIDE AS A COVERING. THE DESIGNS, OR SHAPES, ON THE HIDE SUGGEST HOW IMPORTANT THIS LARGE ANIMAL WAS TO THE CHEYENNE PEOPLE.

GET THE FACTS!

Sometimes, the Cheyenne had to travel a long way to find trees with suitable wood to make poles for their tepees. The smallest tepees used about 12 poles. The largest had 30 or more. Women were often in charge of building them.

CHEYENNE FOOD

The Cheyenne ate different foods depending on their way of life. When they were farmers, they grew crops such as corn, squash, and beans. They fished, hunted small animals, and gathered wild rice, fruits, and roots.

GET THE FACTS!

Bison are the largest land animals in North America. Male bison can be 6.5 feet (2 m) tall and weigh about 2,000 pounds (907 kg). Before white settlers came to the Great Plains, millions of bison lived there. Sometimes, bison are incorrectly called buffalo.

THIS PICTURE SHOWS NATIVE AMERICANS HUNTING BISON ON THE PLAINS IN THE 1800S.

CONTAINER FOR DRIED BISON MEAT

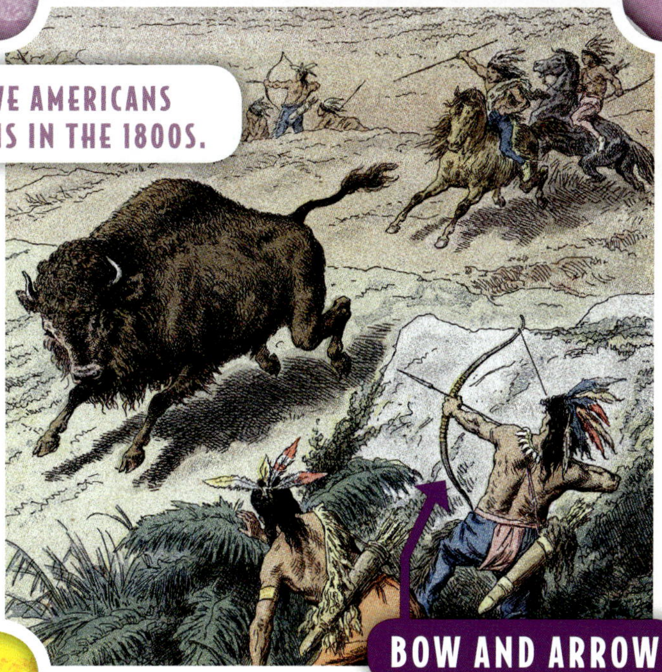

BOW AND ARROW

After the Cheyenne began hunting bison on the Great Plains, bison became their main source of food. The way of hunting bison changed once they got horses and guns from Europeans and other Native Americans. It was easier to follow the bison on horseback than on foot. Deer, elk, antelope, and sheep provided meat too.

THE CHEYENNE LANGUAGE

The Cheyenne people have their own language. It's part of the Algonquian family of languages, which means it's **related** to many other Native American languages. The Cheyenne call themselves Tsétsėhéstȧhese (or Tsitsistas), which is believed to mean "the beautiful people."

GET THE FACTS!

Special marks over letters in the Cheyenne alphabet tell speakers how to say the sounds. For example, á, é, and ó tell us to say these sounds with a high tone, but ȧ, ė, and ȯ should be whispered. A low tone isn't marked.

TRY TO SAY SOME CHEYENNE WORDS. *VEE'E* MEANS TEPEE. *SEMO* MEANS BOAT. *HESE* MEANS FLY.

SAY THE CHEYENNE ALPHABET

A	A SOUND AS IN "FATHER"
E	I SOUND AS IN "PICK"
H	H SOUND AS IN "HAT"
K	K SOUND AS IN "KITE"
'	STOPPING SOUND AS IN "UH-OH"
M	M SOUND AS IN "MAP"
N	N SOUND AS IN "NOT"
O	O SOUND AS IN "NO"
P	P SOUND AS IN "PAN"
S	S SOUND AS IN "SO"
Š	SH SOUND AS IN "SHY"
T	T SOUND AS IN "TAP"
V	V SOUND AS IN "VAN"
X	CH SOUND AS IN "LOCH"

There are only 14 letters in the Cheyenne alphabet. However, a long saying can be said with just one word in Cheyenne. All Cheyenne used the same language, and many even spoke a second or third language. Today, few young people speak Cheyenne, so the language is in danger of dying out.

WHAT THEY WORE

The Cheyenne people made their clothing out of animal skin, such as that of bison, deer, elk, or antelope. Women wore long dresses. Men wore animal-skin cloths around their waists called breechcloths. Women wore leather boots, while men wore flat leather shoes called moccasins. In rain and snow, the Cheyenne kept warm with bison-skin robes and leggings.

A NORTHERN CHEYENNE CHIEF AND HIS DAUGHTER ARE PICTURED HERE IN **TRADITIONAL** CHEYENNE CLOTHING AROUND 1880.

GET THE FACTS!

Fringe sometimes decorated Cheyenne clothing. A fringe is a border or edge made up of hanging strips. As it moved, it helped keep bugs away. Rainwater ran off the ends of fringe so clothing was less wet too.

Beads or porcupine **quills** sometimes decorated clothing. Leaders wore feather headdresses on their head. Warriors wore special shirts into battle called war shirts. Today, many of these items are only worn during special **ceremonies**.

CHEYENNE CHILDREN

Cheyenne children long ago liked the same things the children of today like. They played with toys and enjoyed sports and games. However, instead of going to school, children learned from their elders. Both girls and boys were skilled at riding horses from a young age.

Young boys played with bows and arrows. When they were old enough, they learned hunting, fishing, and fighting.

Young girls played with dolls and toy tepees. They learned to cook, make clothes, and do other chores. Girls sometimes grew up to be warriors and hunters too.

CHEYENNE BOY, AROUND 1900

CHEYENNE GIRL, 1911

GET THE FACTS!

Lacrosse was a popular game among many groups of Native Americans, including the Cheyenne. In this game, players use sticks with long handles and nets for catching, throwing, and carrying a ball. Native Americans sometimes played all day!

LACROSSE WAS PLAYED FOR MANY REASONS. AT TIMES GAMES SETTLED DISPUTES BETWEEN NATIVE PEOPLES INSTEAD OF WAR.

CHEYENNE BANDS AND SOCIETIES

The Cheyenne were once divided into 10 main bands, or groups. They were governed by the **Council** of Forty-four. It was made up of 44 chiefs who made decisions to keep peace among the Cheyenne bands. Seven military societies made choices about going to war. The most famous and powerful of these societies was the Dog Soldiers.

GET THE FACTS!

The Contrary Society was made up of Cheyenne who did many things backward, like moving backwards and saying "yes" when they meant "no." They entertained people and made them laugh. People in this society were thought to help the sick too.

FEATHER HEADDRESS OF THE DOG SOLDIERS

CHEYENNE BANDS WERE MADE UP OF MANY FAMILIES. THIS SOUTHERN CHEYENNE FAMILY IS SHOWN IN 1890.

Cheyenne women belonged to female societies, such as the Quillers' Society in which they decorated important clothing. Other societies focused on different areas of Cheyenne traditional life, such as dance and **medicine**.

THE PLAINS PEOPLES

Many native peoples lived on the Great Plains. That meant that the Cheyenne came across other Plains cultures. The Cheyenne traded bison hides for things they needed from other tribes, such as corn. The Cheyenne were also a key part of the horse trade, helping other peoples get horses.

But the Cheyenne fought with other Native Americans at times. This didn't always mean hurting or killing. Groups sometimes stole horses or guns. The Cheyenne had a tradition called counting coup (KOO). This meant touching an enemy in battle without hurting them.

GET THE FACTS!

Even though the different tribes of the Great Plains didn't always speak the same language, they communicated with each other using a series of hand signals known as Plains sign language (example at left). It was a kind of second language for many.

MANDAN AND CHEYENNE CHIEFS BATTLE, 1833

THERE WERE MANY PEOPLES OF DIFFERENT CULTURES LIVING ON THE GREAT PLAINS, AS YOU CAN SEE FROM THIS MAP.

CHEYENNE ACTIVITIES

The Cheyenne had many chores to do each day to survive. However, they also set aside time for different activities. Making crafts with beads and porcupine quills was popular. They also became famous for carving and decorating pipes.

IN THIS 1832 PAINTING OF CHEYENNE CHIEF WOLF ON THE HILL, YOU CAN SEE A CAREFULLY DECORATED PIPE.

CHEYENNE PIPE CASE WITH QUILLWORK

GET THE FACTS!

Cheyenne **myths** are filled with interesting characters: Hestovatohkeo'o is a deadly creature who looks like a man—with another face on the back of its head! Wihio is a clever spider who plays tricks on people. Mehne is a monster that hides in water.

Storytelling was a way to entertain as well as remember and pass on tales of people and events. People gathered together to hear stories about the past.

Song and dance also helped connect the Cheyenne people. There were many songs about **religion**, nature, love, children, healing, and war.

RELIGION

The Cheyenne religion is **complex**. However, many Cheyenne believed in two main gods: the Wise One Above and a god who lived under the ground. They believed in other spirits as well. The Cheyenne held religious ceremonies and special objects reflected their beliefs.

The most valuable items were four Sacred Arrows and a hat made of bison skin called the Sacred Medicine Hat. Every year, the Cheyenne took part in two of their most important ceremonies: the Renewal of the Sacred Arrows and the Sun Dance. Some Cheyenne still carry on these ceremonies.

THE SUN DANCE WAS A TIME FOR THE CHEYENNE TO CONNECT WITH THEIR RELIGIOUS BELIEFS.

GET THE FACTS!

The Sacred Arrows were said to be found by a Cheyenne man named Sweet Medicine. The feathers of the arrows are replaced each year during the Renewal of the Sacred Arrows ceremony. The 10 Cheyenne bands came together for the ceremony.

CLOTH SHOWING PART OF THE SUN DANCE

CLASHING WITH THE U.S. GOVERNMENT

When white explorers and settlers came into Cheyenne territory, the lives of Native Americans changed. In the 1700s and 1800s, many Cheyenne died of an illness called smallpox, which white settlers and traders brought.

DURING THE SAND CREEK MASSACRE, ABOUT 675 U.S. TROOPS MADE A SURPRISE ATTACK ON A CHEYENNE CAMP THAT HAD ALREADY SURRENDERED. MORE THAN 150 PEOPLE WERE KILLED.

GET THE FACTS!

Black Kettle was a Southern Cheyenne chief who tried to make peace before the Sand Creek Massacre. He later moved to a village on the Washita River where he was killed by Custer's soldiers just four years later.

Fighting between the Cheyenne and the U.S. military began in the 1850s. The Southern Cheyenne tried to make peace with the U.S. government. However, many were killed in surprise attacks, including the Sand Creek **Massacre** of 1864. The Northern Cheyenne helped defeat Lieutenant Colonel George Armstrong Custer and his troops in the Battle of the Little Bighorn in 1876.

ONTO RESERVATIONS

By the 1870s, most Northern and Southern Cheyenne agreed to live on lands set aside by the government called reservations. They were forced to give up traditions. Their children were sent to schools where they could only speak English and had to dress like white children.

GET THE FACTS!

Although they're separated by distance, the Northern and Southern Cheyenne are still in contact and connected by traditions and beliefs. The Northern Cheyenne guard the Sacred Medicine Hat, and the Southern Cheyenne guard the Sacred Arrows.

THE LAND CALLED INDIAN TERRITORY BECAME PART OF THE STATE OF OKLAHOMA IN 1907.

NORTHERN CHEYENNE RESERVATION

- ABOUT 5,000 CHEYENNE
- 444,000 ACRES (1,797 SQ KM)

The Southern Cheyenne went to a reservation in today's Oklahoma, which they shared with the Arapaho. The Northern Cheyenne went there too, but many returned north. Some were killed on the way. President Chester A. Arthur created a reservation for the Northern Cheyenne in Montana in 1884.

THE CHEYENNE TODAY

Over time, the U.S. government allowed the Cheyenne and other Native Americans to govern themselves and reclaim their traditions. Many Cheyenne stayed on reservations, while others live all over the United States.

GET THE FACTS!

The Cheyenne reservations today have schools and businesses. Ranching and farming are some ways the people support themselves. However, the Cheyenne still have to fight to guard their land and resources.

THE RED EARTH FESTIVAL IN OKLAHOMA CITY IS A YEARLY EVENT FOR CHEYENNE AND OTHER NATIVE AMERICANS TO CELEBRATE THEIR RICH CULTURES.

The Cheyenne today have similar clothes, jobs, and homes as other Americans. However, their rich history and culture isn't forgotten. They make sure to practice their traditions. Though few speak the Cheyenne language well, it's now being taught in several schools. With more Cheyenne learning their language and carrying on their ceremonies, the Cheyenne people have a bright future.

GLOSSARY

ceremony An event to honor or celebrate something.

complex Having to do with something with many parts that work together.

council A group of people meant to make decisions for a bigger group.

culture The beliefs and ways of life of a group of people.

entertain To do things that are interesting for people to watch or listen to.

massacre The killing of a large number of people, especially when they cannot defend themselves.

medicine A drug taken to make a sick person well.

myth A story that was told by a people to explain a practice, belief, or natural event.

quill A sharp, stiff point on the body of an animal.

related Connected by family.

religion A belief in and way of honoring a god or gods.

surrender To give up.

traditional Having to do with a long-practiced custom.

FOR MORE INFORMATION

BOOKS

Bodden, Valerie. *Cheyenne*. Mankato, MN: Creative Education, 2020.

Lawton, Cassie M., and Raymond Bial. *The People and Culture of the Cheyenne*. New York, NY: Cavendish Square, 2017.

Maron, Terra Rose. *Cheyenne*. New York, NY: PowerKids Press, 2016.

WEBSITES

Cheyenne Fact Sheet
bigorrin.org/cheyenne_kids.htm
Learn answers to your questions about the Cheyenne people.

The Cheyenne and Arapaho Tribes
cheyenneandarapaho-nsn.gov/project/tribal-history/
Read a short history about how these people came to live together.

Northern Cheyenne Tribe
www.cheyennenation.com
This is the official page for the reservation of this Cheyenne group.

INDEX